CIRCUS PERFORMER

LISA REGAN

WINDMILL
BOOKS™
New York

Published in 2013 by Windmill Books, An Imprint of Rosen Publishing
29 East 21st Street, New York, NY 10010

Produced for Windmill by Calcium Creative Ltd
Editors for Calcium Creative Ltd: Sarah Eason and Vicky Egan
US Editor: Sara Antill
Designer: Nick Leggett

Photo credits: Cover: Shutterstock: Tamas Gerencser bg, Val Thoermer fg.
Inside: Chinese State Circus: Mike Brittian 4; Istockphoto: Rich Legg 19,
Mammamaart 5, Pejft 6, Paco Romero 18; Shutterstock: 3777190317 8,
Helder Almeida 14, Anneka 20, Simone van den Berg 21, Steve Collender
22, Korionov 26, Lanych 3, Litvin Leonid 28, Mojito 27, Claudia Naerdemann
15, Kruglov Orda 25, Losevsky Pavel 7, Photo-oasis 1, 10, Samotrebizan 16,
Shmel 9, 11, Steve Snowden 23, Perov Stanislav 29, Val Thoermer 17, Sandra
van der Steen 12, Lisa F. Young 13; TBWABusted 24.

                    Library of Congress Cataloging-in-Publication Data

Regan, Lisa, 1971–
 Circus performer / by Lisa Regan.
    p. cm. — (Stage school)
 Includes index.
 ISBN 978-1-4488-8093-5 (library binding) — ISBN 978-1-4488-8152-9 (pbk.)
 — ISBN 978-1-4488-8158-1 (6-pack)
 1. Circus—Juvenile literature. 2. Circus performers—Juvenile literature.
 I. Title.
 GV1817.R44 2013
 791.3—dc23
                    2011052813

Manufactured in the United States of America

CPSIA Compliance Information: Batch #B3S12WM: For Further Information contact Windmill Books, New York, New York at 1-866-478-0556

CONTENTS

WELCOME TO THE CIRCUS!

Roll up, roll up! The circus is in town! Get ready for an amazing show full of performances that are designed to surprise and entertain an audience.

Special skills

The people who perform in a circus learn special skills, such as juggling and high-wire walking. Circus **performers** practice their acts for many hours each day until they can put on their show without making any mistakes.

⬇ *The Chinese State Circus has some of the best juggling acts in the world.*

Be a big hit

To keep a circus audience entertained, performers must hold their attention from the very first act they see until it's time to go home. Would you like to have some circus skills? If you put in hours of practice, you, too, could be a big hit.

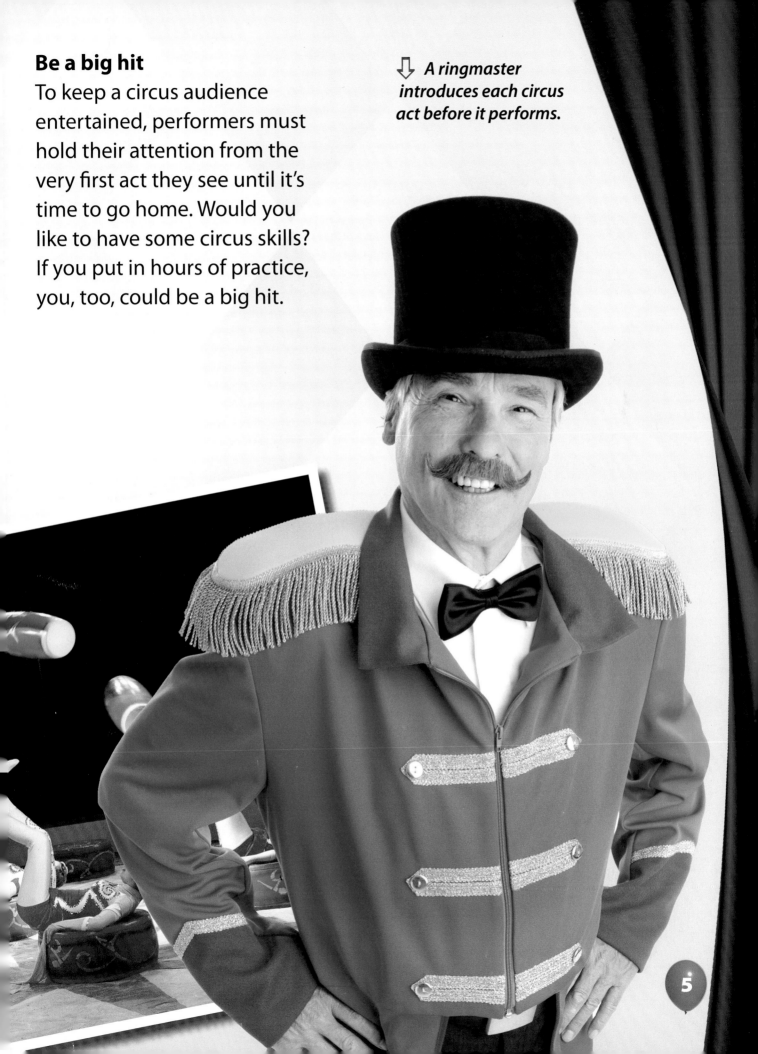

⬇ *A ringmaster introduces each circus act before it performs.*

THE BIG TOP

The people who belong to a circus travel with their show from place to place. When they arrive at each site, they put up a large, colorful tent, called a big top. The circus show is held inside the big top.

No talking!

Usually, circus performers do not speak during their act. They remain quiet because they need to put all of their energy into performing. Exciting music is played during the performance, which helps to keep the audience entertained.

⇩ *A big top tent is often brightly colored.*

In the ring

The big top stage is called a ring because of its shape. It was designed in a circle so that horses could gallop around it while riders stood on their backs.

Your big top

Your first show will be at home, not in a big top. Clear a space in the center of the room. Set some chairs or cushions in a circle for the audience. Ask an adult to help you hang up some brightly colored drapes or silks to set the scene.

⇧ *The crowd sits in a circle in the big top so that everyone can see the act being performed.*

CLASS CLOWN!

Everyone loves circus clowns! They make the audience laugh, have lots of fun playing off other clowns, and get to dress up in the craziest costumes!

happy character clown

Auguste clown

sad character clown

What kind of clown are you?

Did you know that there is more than one type of circus clown?

- A **whiteface clown** is the leader of the group. He tries to keep the other clowns in line.

- A character clown may be a butcher, baker, housewife, or hobo.

- An **Auguste clown** (or red clown) is a really goofy clown!

IN THE SPOTLIGHT

Be inspired!

There are lots of famous clown characters in movies that you can look to for inspiration. Check out movies by **Laurel and Hardy**, the **Marx Brothers**, and **Charlie Chaplin** to see these great **slapstick** characters in action.

⇐ *Wear a crazy-looking wig if you choose to be an Auguste clown!*

DRESSED FOR LAUGHS

It's easy to spot clowns by their colorful clothes, wigs, and big, red noses. If you want to be a clown, choose brightly colored clothes with spotted, checkered, and striped patterns. Add colorful buttons and striped or checkered scarves.

⇧ *All the best clowns have a pair of comic shoes!*

IN THE SPOTLIGHT

Bozo the Clown

One of the best-known clowns is Bozo, who famously wore really huge shoes, size 83 AAA! Many different people have played the part of Bozo.

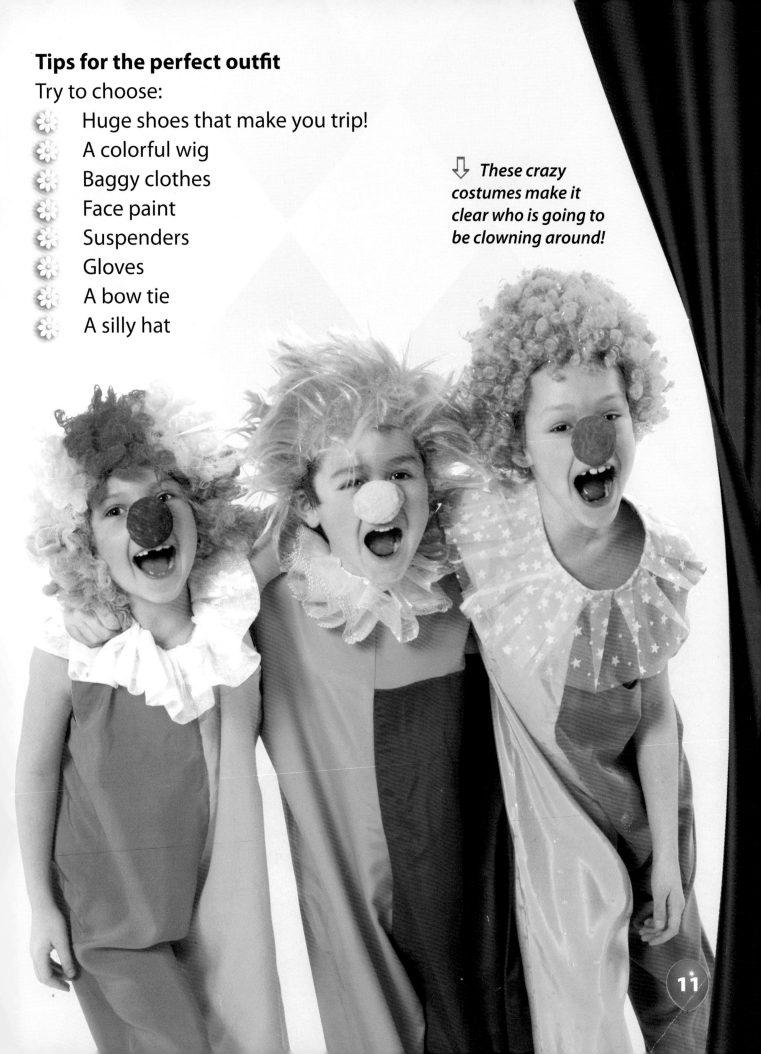

Tips for the perfect outfit

Try to choose:

- Huge shoes that make you trip!
- A colorful wig
- Baggy clothes
- Face paint
- Suspenders
- Gloves
- A bow tie
- A silly hat

⬇ *These crazy costumes make it clear who is going to be clowning around!*

11

CLOWNING AROUND

Circus clowns make the crowd laugh with their funny acts. Many wear hats or bow ties that suddenly flash and spin, and their noses light up, too. Sometimes a clown pulls out a toy gun that pops out a flag printed with the word "BANG!" to make the audience laugh.

⇐ *You can use colorful balloons and umbrellas to get extra laughs!*

BE A STAR

Got you!

The simplest jokes are often the best. Go to shake hands with someone in the audience, but instead of letting them grip your hand, put your thumb on the end of your nose and wave your fingers at them!

Watch out!

Clowning usually ends up messy, with plenty of slipping on banana peels, throwing cream pies in faces, tipping buckets of water over heads, and tying everyone in knots with lots of silly string. Save this for the big top, not your den!

⬇ *Lean too close to a clown and he may squirt you with water from his hat!*

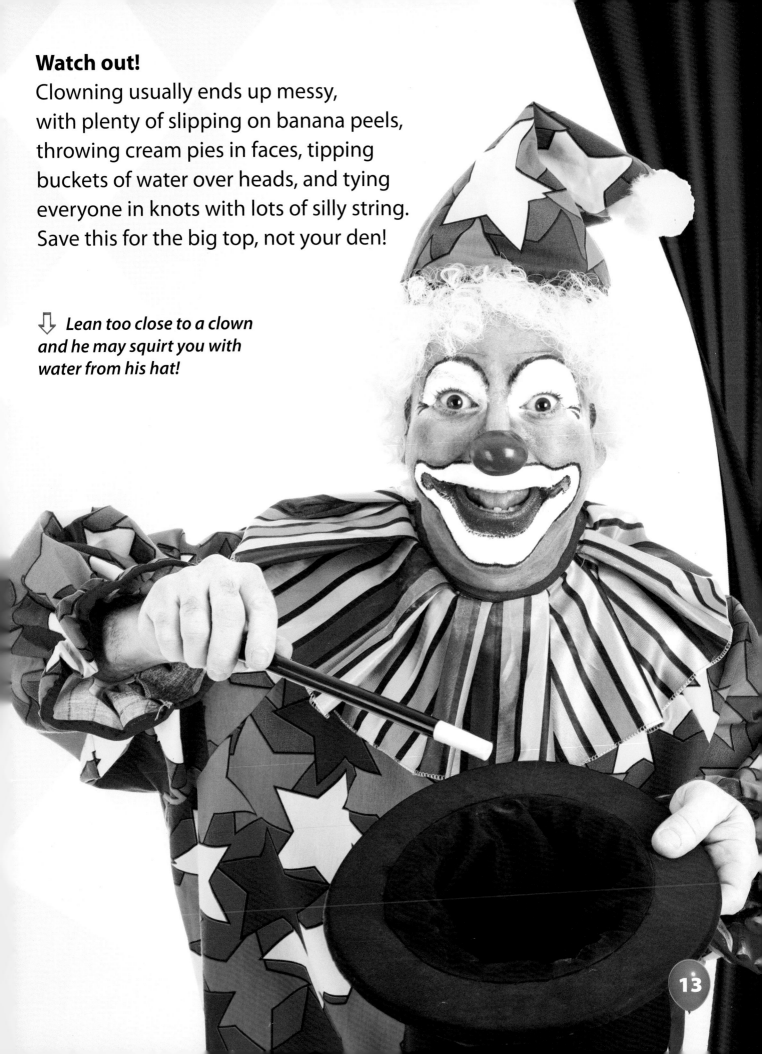

JUGGLING ACT

Can you juggle? If not, it's time to learn! The most skilled jugglers shock the crowd by juggling with knives, swords, fire, and even chainsaws! You should never try to juggle any of these items, though. Your fingers are too important!

Learning the skill

The best jugglers make juggling look really easy, but it isn't. You will need to:

- Practice for many hours to learn how to juggle well.
- Start juggling with scarves. These fall slowly, which makes it easier for you to master your skills.
- Move on to balls when you can confidently juggle with scarves.

➡ *Use brightly colored balls for your act.*

⬇ *Once you can juggle with balls, try out some colored juggling rings.*

BE A STAR

Oranges and lemons

Practice juggling with different things. You will wow your friends if you can grab some fruits from a bowl and juggle them without dropping them.

FACE PAINT

Clowns paint their faces to look either happy or sad. Take a look at some clown faces, and then try painting your own clown face. You could try a happy face and a sad one, too.

↑ *Pierrot is a male character but lots of females play him, too.*

Mime faces

A well-known clown character named **Pierrot** has a dreamy, white face, with a teardrop under one eye. Pierrot is played by a **mime** artist, so he never speaks. Instead, he tells his story through movement. To create a sad look, try painting your face like Pierrot, too.

BE A STAR

Paint your face

❀ Paint a red line around your mouth. Make it point up at the ends for a smile and down for a sad face.

❀ Paint a thick, white band around the red line.

❀ Add a blue or black line around the white band.

❀ Next, paint a thick, white band around or above your eyes.

❀ Paint on eyebrows (they can be higher than your real eyebrows.)

❀ Finish with red cheeks and lips.

⇧ *You can paint a happy clown face if you like.*

MAGICAL FACES

If you want to be a circus **acrobat**, it is very important to make the crowd concentrate on your movements. For this reason, circus acrobats often wear bright colors and dramatic makeup. Before you perform your act, you could paint your face with a special design.

Wear pale lipstick.

Clip back your hair.

Add lots of glitter.

BE A STAR

Sparkle and color

Acrobats and **trapeze artists** wear tight-fitting, sparkly costumes in bright colors. Use these colors in your face-painting design. Try painting a butterfly's wing on each side of your nose. Add plenty of glitter and sparkle for some extra circus magic!

⇧ *Paint your face to look like a dragon or a tiger!*

Animal faces

Not all circuses today have performing animals, but you could be a stand-in! Paint your face and put on a "big cat" show. Leap through a hoop and spring across the floor, just like a big cat!

FORTUNE-TELLING

Some circuses have sideshows that take place in tents smaller than the big top. These shows may include a fortune-teller. This is a person who claims they can see what will happen in the future.

⬇ *Some fortune-tellers read your palm.*

Palm readers

A palm reader looks at how long and deep the lines are on the front, or palm, of your hand. This tells the palm reader how healthy and happy she thinks you are going to be.

Crystal ball

Some fortune-tellers look into a crystal ball to tell the future. They claim that within the crystal ball they can see a picture of something that will happen to you in the future.

⇧ *Fortune-tellers say they can see your future in a crystal ball!*

BALLOON MODELING

How do you conjure up a giraffe, a dog, or a crazy hat if you aren't a magician? You learn balloon modeling, that's how! You can create lots of different objects and animals from balloons, which will impress your audience.

BE A STAR

Give it a twist!

Balloon modeling isn't difficult to learn. It is a great skill to have and will make your own act more fun. Look online to see how to do it, then start practicing your twists and think how to work balloon modeling into your performance.

⇐ *Make your audience gasp with the coolest balloon creatures.*

Meeting the crowd

Many clowns know how to twist and turn a balloon into cool shapes. It's a great way for them to put a smile on the faces of their younger fans. This may be one of the few times that a clown breaks his silence. He will often have a funny story to tell while he's modeling.

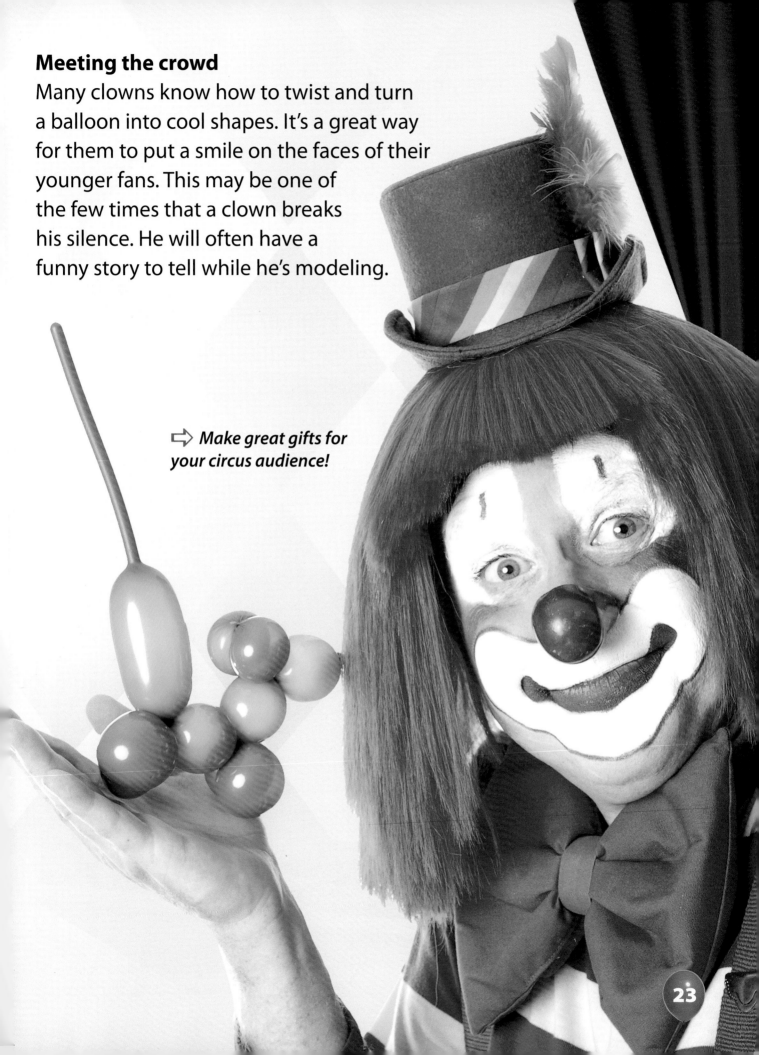

➡ *Make great gifts for your circus audience!*

TAKING A TUMBLE

Clowns make us laugh, but acrobats make us gasp. Their bodies are very strong and bendable, and they can balance on just about anything! Acrobats thrill the circus audience with one of the most exciting acts seen in the big top.

⬆ *Cirque du Soleil performers are some of the most exciting acrobats in the world.*

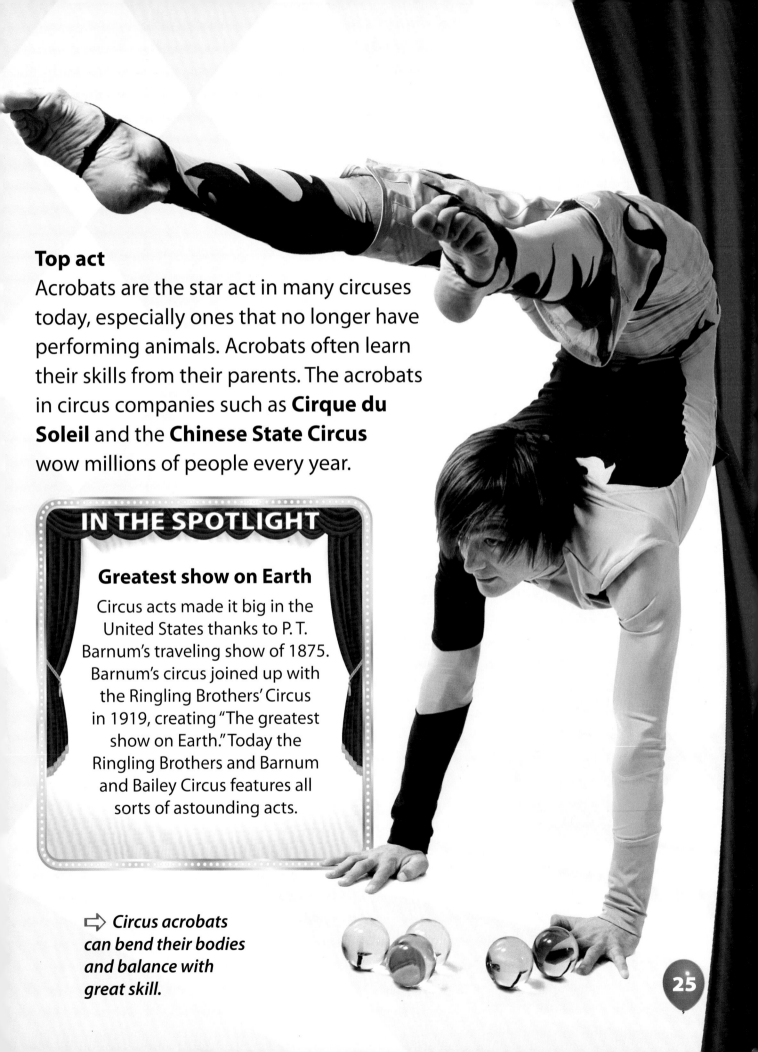

Top act

Acrobats are the star act in many circuses today, especially ones that no longer have performing animals. Acrobats often learn their skills from their parents. The acrobats in circus companies such as **Cirque du Soleil** and the **Chinese State Circus** wow millions of people every year.

IN THE SPOTLIGHT

Greatest show on Earth

Circus acts made it big in the United States thanks to P. T. Barnum's traveling show of 1875. Barnum's circus joined up with the Ringling Brothers' Circus in 1919, creating "The greatest show on Earth." Today the Ringling Brothers and Barnum and Bailey Circus features all sorts of astounding acts.

➡ *Circus acrobats can bend their bodies and balance with great skill.*

LOST FOR WORDS

Who's that clownlike character with a sad, white face and black-and-white clothes? It's a mime artist, telling a story without saying a word. Watch carefully and you'll see just how much a person can say without ever talking.

Bip the Clown

French mime artist Marcel Marceau, who died in 2007, invented a famous silent character named Bip the Clown. Through Bip, Marceau helped to make mime popular all over the world.

⇐ *Mime artists use movements to "talk" to the audience.*

A mime artist's makeup, gloves, and costume make the audience notice his or her movements more.

Watch yourself!

Stand in front of a mirror and look at your face. Wipe your hand down your face and look sad. Next, wipe your hand upward and smile. That's your very first mime! Now, pretend to climb an imaginary ladder. See how hard it is to make your mime look real!

DON'T TRY THIS AT HOME!

It's great to play the clown or to practice acrobatics, but some circus acts should *not* be tried at home! You can enjoy watching these acts at the circus, but do not try them yourself.

Thrilling acts

Many people love the thrill of watching fire-eaters, high-wire walkers, and trapeze artists flying through the air. These performers spend years learning their skills and months putting together their acts to make them as safe as possible.

⬇ *A fire performer pushes his skills to the limit to keep the audience gasping for more.*

⬇ *Some acrobats hang on silks, like ballet dancers in the air.*

IN THE SPOTLIGHT

Human cannonball

In a human cannonball act, a person is fired out of a special cannon and must land safely in a net. Many people have died performing this act.

GLOSSARY

acrobat

(A-kruh-bat) A performer who does daring gymnastic moves and balancing acts.

Auguste clown

(ah-GOOST KLOWN) Also known as a red clown, this is the clumsiest clown. He trips, falls over, and plays pranks.

Charlie Chaplin

(CHAR-lee CHA-plin) An English comic actor and director, famous for making silent movies in the early 1900s.

Chinese State Circus

(chy-NEEZ STAYT SUR-kus) A touring circus of Chinese acrobats. Their skills date back more than 2,000 years.

Cirque du Soleil

(SURK DOO soh-LAY) A Canadian company of performers that mixes circus arts with street entertainment.

Laurel and Hardy

(LOR-ul AND HAR-dee) A comedy act featuring Stan Laurel and Oliver Hardy.

Marx Brothers

(MARKS BRUH-therz) A comedy act mainly featuring the three brothers Chico, Harpo, and Groucho Marx. They were successful on stage and in the movies from the early 1900s to about 1950.

mime

(MYM) To act out an idea or mood using movements instead of words.

performers

(per-FAWR-merz) People who entertain an audience.

Pierrot

(PEE-uh-row) A sad clown, usually a mime artist.

slapstick

(SLAP-stik) A type of comedy in which people chase, bump into, and play jokes on each other.

trapeze artists

(tra-PEEZ AR-tists) Circus performers who do amazing gymnastics on a trapeze, which is a bar that hangs like a swing high up above the ring in a big top.

whiteface clown

(WYT-fays) A clown who is more serious than the rest of his group. He is often the group's leader.

FURTHER READING

Cassidy, John, and B. C. Rimbeaux. *Juggling for the Complete Klutz*. New York: Klutz, 2007.

Fleming, Candace. *The Great and Only Barnum: The Tremendous, Stupendous Life of Showman P. T. Barnum*. New York: Schwartz & Wade, 2009.

Meinking, Mary. *Who Walks the Tightrope?: Working at a Circus*. Wild Work. Chicago: Heinemann-Raintree, 2010.

Robertson, Patrisha. *Cirque du Soleil: Parade of Colors*. New York: Abrams, 2003.

Spielman, Gloria. *Marcel Marceau: Master of Mime*. Minneapolis, MN: Kar-Ben Publishing, 2011.

WEBSITES

For web resources related to the subject of this book, go to: www.windmillbooks.com/weblinks and select this book's title.

INDEX